STRATEGIC MINDSET

A 7-DAY PLAN TO IDENTIFY WHAT MATTERS
AND CREATE A STRATEGY THAT WORKS

THIBAUT MEURISSE

CONTENTS

WHO IS THIS BOOK FOR?

Do you keep hustling without having much result to show for it? Do you feel overwhelmed and unable to find the most effective task to focus on? Do you buy into the myth you must work harder to be successful?

In truth, doing more is often not the solution. Productivity is pointless without a highly effective strategy. This is why you must become obsessed with thinking strategically. Just as you have to think several moves ahead to win a chess game, you must practice thinking months, years, or even decades ahead to win at the productivity game. With the correct strategic thinking, you can save years and achieve many more of your goals than would otherwise be the case.

In other words, you must develop what I call "strategic productivity". Each move you make must be impactful. And you must be constantly on the lookout for the one move that could leapfrog your success and massively improve your life.

So, are you interested in learning more about strategic productivity?

This book, *Strategic Mindset*, is for you if you:

- Keep hustling without getting the results you want,
- Feel overwhelmed, not knowing what to focus on to achieve your goals,
- Lack clarity regarding your goals, or
- Keep studying more but fail to take enough concrete action.

If any of the above seems familiar and you want to learn how to become a strategic producer, read on.

Your Free Step-By-Step Workbook

To help develop a highly effective strategy to achieve your goals, I've created a workbook as a companion guide to his book. Make sure you download it at the following URL:

https://whatispersonaldevelopment.org/strategic-mindset

If you have any difficulties downloading the workbook contact me at:

thibaut.meurisse@gmail.com

and I will send it to you as soon as possible.

Alternatively, you can also use the workbook available at the end of this book

Boost your productivity now with The Productivity Series

This book is the fourth book in the "**Productivity Series**". You can check out the other books in the series at the URL below:

mybook.to/productivity-series

INTRODUCTION

In today's society, everyone is obsessed with doing more. Being busy has become a badge of honor. We want to show the people around us how productive we are. We want our neighbors to see how much busier we are than everyone else.

However, many of us misunderstand productivity. While we may be busy on the surface, we often accomplish very little. Adding more things to our never-ending to-do list doesn't necessarily make us more productive. In some cases, it has the opposite effect. Using the latest productivity app doesn't help much either. While technologies such as the internet are a wonderful source of information, or a way to learn new skills, to be effective, they must be used tactically.

People like Benjamin Franklin or Leonardo Da Vinci didn't have all the productivity tools we now have, yet they were far more productive than most people today. What does this say about productivity as we see it these days?

In this book, we'll define productivity and see how you can achieve more in less time. The goal is to turn you into a strategic producer in just seven days. To help you reach this goal, every day you'll be asked to answer questions and complete simple exercises.

More specifically, in *Strategic Mindset*, you'll discover how to:

- Use the power of long-term thinking to achieve more than you can imagine,
- Learn the right skills and develop your talents the correct way,
- Plan your year for maximum effectiveness,
- Stop being efficient and become effective instead (and why it matters),
- Think smartly to make every action you take impactful, and
- Find the right information and learn faster and better than everybody around you.

If any of the above piques your interest, read on.

WHAT IS STRATEGIC PRODUCTIVITY

Throughout this book, I'll use the terms "strategic productivity" and "strategic producer". Before we start, let's define them briefly.

Strategic productivity means using your time in a way that enables you to achieve maximum results with minimum effort. It means making sure that whatever you're working on at any point in time is connected to your overall vision. There is nothing more wasteful than spending time on a task that didn't need to be done in the first place. As such, to become a strategic producer you must (among other things):

- Develop clarity regarding your long-term vision,
- Identify the best strategy to achieve your goals as quickly and effectively as possible,
- Develop the ability to ask yourself the right questions,
- Cultivate the ability to focus and avoid jumping from one thing to the next, and
- Learn to approach any task the most effective way possible.

In this book, we'll cover the following:

In **Part I. Planning Effectively**, we'll see how to plan effectively and how to identify the key tasks you must focus on to boost your productivity. On **Day 1**, you'll learn to plan your year for maximum effectiveness. On **Day 2**, you'll work on identifying your most impactful actions. And on **Day 3**, you'll flesh out your next 90 days.

In **Part II. Effectiveness vs. Efficiency**, we'll discover how to become truly effective each day. You'll be introduced to a powerful 7-Step Process that will ensure you approach each task the correct way and achieve tangible results (**Day 4**).

In **Part III. Thinking Smart**, you'll learn how to improve your thinking to enhance your focus and get the most out of each action you take. As you practice thinking more strategically, you'll improve your overall results significantly (**Day 5**).

In **Part IV. Learning Effectively**, you'll discover how to find the right information and absorb it as quickly and effectively as possible. You'll also discover common learning mistakes and how to avoid them (**Day 6**).

Finally, in **Part V. Managing Your Energy**, we'll discuss how to make the most of the energy you have available each day. We'll see how to leverage your peak energy to achieve more and how to segment your day for optimal results (**Day 7**).

Are you ready?

PART I

PLANNING EFFECTIVELY

You cannot hit a target you don't set. Strategic productivity is impossible without a certain level of clarity regarding your needs and goals, and without a plan to achieve them. Yet how many people lack a clear vision? How many people forget what they're actually trying to achieve, hustling every day without questioning the path they're travelling?

The management consultant, Peter Drucker, once said that efficiency is doing things right while effectiveness is doing the right things. There is no point doing things right if those things don't move you closer to your goals.

In this section, we're going to discuss the importance of planning strategically to ensure that you work on the right things each day. Strategic productivity is not about doing *more*, it's about doing less of the things that bring little results.

Note that, in this book, we'll focus mostly on one major goal. Once you understand the process, you will be able to apply the same method for any other future goal.

1. The power of long-term thinking

Your ability to think long term is one of the best predictors of success. Why? Because setting long-term goals means saying no to an infinite number of possibilities. By removing options, you can direct all your energy toward achieving your goals. Once you know where you want to go, you can reverse-engineer the steps you need to take to reach your destination. As a result, each action you take will become more impactful.

When you play chess, your goal is to win. To do so, you have to anticipate your opponent's moves. Strategic productivity is a similar process. You anticipate potential roadblocks and identify key moves. You strive to make each action impactful. Everything you do is linked to the future you want to create. As such, it is no surprise that people who spend time every day thinking of where they want to be in five years obtain better results than those who don't.

What about you? Do you think strategically, or are you merely showing up each day with no clear strategy or action plan to follow?

2. The power of compounding

Another benefit of strategic productivity is that it unleashes the power of compounding. When you keep making progress toward your goals each day, you build momentum. You accumulate small wins, which boost your confidence and increase your motivation. Each new day builds on the previous one. While results may not be apparent at the beginning, soon enough you will reach a tipping point. Things start to accelerate, and your success becomes exponential.

In his book *Atomic Habits*, James Clear writes that if you get just one percent better every day, over a year you'll be thirty-seven times more effective.

Of course, this is only theoretical, but I'm sure you get the point.

The bottom line is, to build momentum and activate the power of compounding, you need to focus on a very few things consistently over a long enough period of time.

3. The power of focus

As Bruce Lee is quoted as saying, *"I fear not the man who has practiced 10,000 kicks once, but I fear the man who has practiced one kick 10,000 times."*

When you work toward your most important goals each day, you activate the power of focus. And with enough focus, you can achieve almost anything you desire. As I wrote in *Master Your Focus*:

"Focus acts like an ax. If you try to cut down a tree by hitting it in thousands of different spots, you'll never succeed. But when you focus and hit the same spot over and over, you can cut down even the biggest tree. With laser-sharp focus you can achieve almost anything you desire."

The first scenario is what most people do. They try to fell a tree by hitting a different spot each time. It's no wonder, then, that these people fail to reach their goals. For instance, someone who learns karate will improve faster if they practice every day. However, if their training is erratic or if they try to learn tae kwon do, jujitsu and aikido simultaneously, their progress will be severely restricted. As a youngster, Michael Jordan loved both basketball and baseball but, eventually, he had to choose one sport. Had he chosen both, he would probably never have become a world-renowned basketball superstar.

This metaphor applies to many things we do throughout our lives. When you pursue two rabbits, you end up catching none, or a bird in the hand really is worth two in the bush.

In short, strategic productivity involves hitting a tree in the same spot until it falls down. It requires that you:

1. Focus on only a few goals at the same time,
2. Implement a sound strategy to reach them, and
3. Make progress towards these goals each day by taking action in line with your strategy.

DAY 1—PLANNING YOUR YEAR

Most people spend more time planning a one-week vacation than they spend planning their life.

— MICHAEL HYATT, AUTHOR AND SPEAKER.

Today, we're going to work on planning your year. This will help you unleash the power of strategic productivity. So, what would you like to accomplish in the upcoming twelve months? What really excites you? What would make a huge difference in your professional or personal life?

As we've already mentioned, the more clarity you have the better. To plan your year, start by brainstorming ideas using the question below:

What would make the next twelve months truly valuable?

Spend five to ten minutes writing down answers to this question.

Then, to further help you, visualize yourself exactly twelve months from today. Now, write down what you would have accomplished by filling in the prompt below using your action guide:

The last twelve months were truly amazing because...

Finally, spend a moment visualizing your achievement, while experiencing a deep feeling of satisfaction from achieving it.

Now that you've written down some of the things you'd like to achieve, select just one of them. This will make it easier for you to develop strategic productivity. To help you identify the one thing you'd like to focus on, answer the following questions:

- If I can achieve one thing this year, which one would make me the proudest?
- If I can achieve one thing this year, which one would make the biggest positive difference in my life?
- What's the one thing I've always wanted to do (but haven't)?
- What do I really, really want in life?
- What's the one thing that scares me the most? (The thing that scares you is often the thing you need to do the most.)

If you need more help refining your vision, refer to the previous book in this series, Book 3, *Powerful Focus*.

Action step

Using your action guide, plan the next twelve months.

DAY 2—MAKING THE DOMINOS FALL

You need to be doing fewer things for more effect instead of doing more things with side effects.

— GARY KELLER, AUTHOR OF *THE ONE THING*.

In truth, there is an almost infinite number of actions you can take to move from Point A—where you are now—to Point B—where you want to be. Your task here is to narrow down these options and identify the actions with the biggest leverage possible. Remember, you need to hit your big tree in the same spot with your ax every time before you'll be able to shout, "Timber!". This will be the best use of your time and energy.

Now, look at the primary goal you identified on Day 1. What dominos need to fall for you to reach that goal? What impactful actions will move the needle the most effectively? Brainstorm ideas, using your action guide. A sound strategy will save you a great deal of time—sometimes years. Conversely, a poor strategy will lead you to waste your time and energy, and reduce the chances of reaching your goal.

Bear in mind that oftentimes, the first ideas you come up with aren't always the best ones. But when you spend time thinking about it, you'll likely produce great answers. The success expert, Brian Tracy, recommends writing at least twenty actions we can take to reach our goal. He also suggests that the last idea is often the most effective. Later in this book, we'll discuss in greater depth how to find the right dominos. So, if you're unsure yet, don't worry.

So, what are the right dominos for you?

Here are some characteristics of the right dominos:

1. They help you **build momentum** and activate the power of compounding,
2. They entail a **paradigm shift** that changes your reality immediately and improves your results,
3. They allow you to make **significant progress** toward your goals, and/or
4. They dramatically **reduce your options**, eliminating most of the irrelevant actions you could be taking to reach your goal.

1. They help you build momentum

The right domino enables you to generate momentum and stay motivated so that you can move toward your goal consistently. In other words, the right domino can be called a "daily habit".

For instance, let's say your goal is to learn how to play the piano. Then, your domino might be to carve out time each day to practice. If you practice every day, progress over time is inevitable.

Or let's say your goal is to learn Spanish. Then, your domino might be to practice for thirty minutes each day, using an app like Duolingo.

What about you? What dominos could help you reach your goal? If you were to implement one new daily habit, which one would most improve your chance of attaining your goal? And how do you know this?

2. They entail a paradigm shift

Sometimes, the most effective way to achieve your goal is to adopt a new paradigm. After all, if you were already using the correct paradigm, you would have reached your goal already, wouldn't you?

Now, what is a paradigm? In short, a paradigm is a model of reality based on a set of assumptions or hypotheses. The more accurate your paradigms are, the more effective your actions will be, and the better results you'll obtain. A paradigm shift can be defined as a change of perception. A paradigm shift occurs when you ask yourself different questions and gain new insights and change your behavior as a result. A new paradigm often requires that you take a step back and look at the overall picture. It requires you to challenge some of your most deeply ingrained assumptions.

We can sum it up as follows:

Accurate thinking —> effective actions —> tangible results.

Conversely:

Inaccurate thinking —> ineffective actions —> mediocre/inconsistent results.

For example, an aspiring writer may spend most of their time sending query letters to publishers. The assumption is that they need to find a publisher. However, by taking a step back, they may realize there is another option—they can self-publish their books. Suddenly, there is no longer any need to send query letters. There's no need to wait months or years to publish their books either. Instead, they can publish their books as soon as they are ready. Although self-publishing may not be for everyone, it can definitely accelerate things. In this case, working toward becoming an independent, self-published author is a paradigm shift.

Here's another example. You may have built your identity around the concept of hard work (hustling). While there is nothing wrong with working hard, you may learn that hustling is not the most effective way to reach your goals. In many cases, you will obtain better results by zeroing in on key tasks, while eliminating non-critical ones.

Now, review your goal and try to create a paradigm shift by changing the way you perceive it. Use some of the following questions to guide you:

- What's the fastest way to achieve my goal?
- If I were lazy and wanted to do as little work as possible, what would I do to achieve my goal quickly and effectively?
- What would Albert Einstein, Bill Gates, or Elon Musk do to achieve the same goal?
- What if this goal is not the right one for me? What if there's a goal that better meets my needs and is more closely aligned with my values?
- Can I reframe my goal? If so, how?

3. They allow you to make significant progress toward your goal

By making the right dominos fall, you can achieve your goals much faster. In some cases, toppling the right domino may be a hundred times more effective than anything else you could be doing instead. Thus, you need to keep looking for specific actions or strategies that could multiply your progress.

As Garry Keller wrote in *The One Thing*, "*In 2001, I called a meeting of our key executive team. As fast as we were growing, we were still not acknowledged by the very top people in our industry. I challenged our group to brainstorm one hundred ways to turn this situation around. It took us all day to come up with the list. The next morning, we narrowed the list down to ten ideas, and from there we chose just one big idea. The one that we decided on was that we would write a book on how to become an elite performer in our industry. It worked. Eight years later, that one book had not only become a national bestseller, but also had morphed into a series of books with total sales of over a million copies. In an industry of about a million people, one thing changed our image forever."*

For me, as a writer, the correct domino was simply to write more books in the same niche, and in a consistent manner. For Hal Elrod, author of *The Miracle Morning*, his domino was to give a couple of hundred podcast interviews in the twelve months following the release of his book.

Of course, in practice, we seldom—if ever—do just one thing, but there is often one specific strategy that, when executed properly, will dramatically increase our results. Your job is to discover the perfect strategy for you.

Even when we hustle our way to success, it is almost always the case that only a minority of our actions lead to tangible results. We simply didn't take the time to identify what these specific successful actions were. Look at one accomplishment you achieved in the past. Perhaps, you've completed a major project. Perhaps, you achieved a major personal goal or mastered a new skill. Now, did you complete that project, reach that goal, or master that skill *because* you worked so hard, or *in spite* of it? If you were to start all over again, what would you do differently? What would you do stop doing? What would you do more of?

Let's be realistic though. In most cases, we need to experiment with different approaches before we can find the right one for us. However, you must remember that you are almost always doing too many separate things. I've yet to meet someone who is *too* focused, but I've met many who are out of focus.

What about you? What domino needs to fall for you to reach your major goal?

4. They dramatically reduce your options

A sound strategy is not just about what to do, it is also, and perhaps most importantly, about what *not* to do. If you try to do everything, it means you have no clear strategy. It means you aren't thinking hard enough. Anybody can hustle, but not everybody can think hard enough to make sure they tackle the right tasks. Or, as I like to say, "Busyness is laziness in thinking" (although, I'm pretty sure I read it somewhere).

The point is this. A good strategy must narrow your options. It will allow you to develop laser-sharp focus and ensure that your actions are truly impactful.

Narrowing down before expanding

Interestingly, most of the largest companies in the world started with a narrow approach. For example:

- Amazon started by selling books online and expanded to become the world's largest online retailer. Amazon now offers cloud services (AWS) to numerous companies and generates billions of dollars every year with its ad platform.
- Google strived to create the best search engine possible before going into video content (YouTube), ads (Google/YouTube ads), robotics, self-driving cars, and much more.
- Apple started with the personal computer before successfully venturing into audio players (iPod),

smartphones (iPhone), tablets (iPad), TV Services (iTV), and so on.

- Virgin started by selling records, but its founder, Richard Branson, now manages over 400 companies.

More interestingly, even though Amazon started by selling books online, Jeff Bezos already had a clear vision for his company. His goal was for Amazon to become the *Everything Store*—a platform on which customers and sellers would come together. Ultimately, he wanted customers to be able to buy almost anything they desired on Amazon. But he started with what he thought would be the easiest item to sell online—books. Then, he kept adding more and more products. In short, at first, he narrowed his approach and dominated a smaller market, and then, he expanded over time. This is how most companies grow, because it is almost impossible to dominate an entire industry from scratch.

You can apply a similar approach to your personal or professional goals. Narrow your options either by niching down, reducing the number of products or services you offer, or limiting the scope of your goals to make them less overwhelming. Such an approach comes with the following benefits:

- It forces you to clarify your goals,
- It enables you to have tangible results faster, which boosts your confidence and motivation,
- It limits the amount of time, effort, and resources needed to make progress, and
- It lowers your resistance by making your goal(s) less daunting.

For example, when I decided to become a full-time writer, I chose to go the self-publishing road and focus exclusively on Amazon. My strategy was simply to release books in the same niche consistently month after month, year after year. By following this specific strategy, I purposefully said no to various activities such as:

- Coaching clients,
- Creating training courses,
- Doing podcast interviews,
- Holding seminars, or
- Selling books on other platforms (e.g., Kobo, Apple, Google Play).

Paradoxically, focusing most of my time and effort on writing books allowed me to gain traction with the Amazon algorithm, which opened up new opportunities. With this extra boost of visibility, I:

- Received offers from publishers and sold the foreign rights of several of my books in countries such as Russia, Brazil, India, Japan, Portugal, Serbia, and Vietnam,
- Received invitations to speak on numerous podcasts, and
- Received emails from readers asking whether I offered coaching services.

In a sense, writing books consistently in a specific niche became my ONE thing. It made almost everything else easier or unnecessary.

One of my friends tried to land a publishing deal for years. Being unsuccessful, he traveled along the self-publishing road instead. A few years later, as he became a successful author, he was able to sell the foreign rights of his books in over a dozen countries. And, this time, he didn't even have to contact publishers first—they contacted him!

The point is, some strategies, when executed successfully, can greatly accelerate your success.

What about you? How could you narrow your options? And what single action could dramatically reduce your options and enable you to make incredible progress toward your goal?

* * *

Action step

Using your action guide, identify the right dominos you need to topple to maximize your odds of reaching your goal. Ask yourself the following questions:

- What single repeated action would enable me to build the most momentum?
- What new paradigm(s) could I adopt?
- What specific strategy would have the biggest possible impact and allow me to make the greatest progress?
- What one thing would reduce my field of options and make almost everything else easier or unnecessary?

DAY 3—PLANNING YOUR 90 DAYS

The best thing about the future is that it comes one day at
a time.

— Abraham Lincoln, former President of the United
States.

Now that you have selected the specific goal to focus on this year,
you can begin to reverse-engineer the process that will allow you
to achieve it.

Often, people set goals at the beginning of the year as part of their
New Year's resolutions, but we all know what happens next, right?
They give up on them after only a few weeks at best. Instead of
setting yearly goals, I recommend you focus most of your attention
on the next 90 days.

Why 90 days?

Because 90 days is the perfect length of time to make tremendous
progress toward your goals. At the same time, it's not so far in the

future that it makes your goals too distant or too vague. Conversely, you can almost see the finish line.

We can summarize the benefits of setting 90-day goals as follows:

- **They make your goals more tangible.** Having implemented specific milestones, your goals will become much more real. You can see them more vividly, which motivates you to take the necessary action.
- **They force you to create a more detailed blueprint.** Having little time to reach your goals, you have to refine your plan and identify the key tasks more precisely.
- **They create a sense of urgency.** You don't have much time and must ensure you're making progress toward these goals every day. You have no time to slack off.
- **They encourage you to measure your progress more consistently.** You have to check that you're on track to hit each milestone more often.

For instance, you can set a goal of losing five pounds of excess weight in the next 90 days instead of twenty pounds over the whole year. This goal looks much more tangible and within your reach. And as you further break it down and create a specific plan, it will become even more realistic.

Writing a book is another good example. If you give yourself 90 days instead of a full year to complete your book, you'll immediately feel a sense of urgency. To make it happen, you'll have to break down the goal and create a fairly detailed process. This, in turn, will make your goals even more tangible. Having no time to waste, you're more likely to start right away.

Now, you don't necessarily need to set overly challenging 90-day goals. Just setting 90-day goals will ensure you move toward your biggest ambitions or dreams, because 90 days is always enough time to make tremendous progress toward any of your endeavors.

Action step

Using your action guide, set your 90 goals as below:

First, look at your yearly goal and identify the milestones you must hit to reach it. Reverse-engineer the process. To do so, ask yourself the following questions:

"What would I need to have completed by the third quarter of the year to ensure I'll hit my target by the end of the fourth?"

"What about the second and first quarters?"

Write down the key milestones for each quarter with as much detail as possible. Don't try to create a perfect plan, just do your best. If necessary, you can refine the process along the way.

PART II

EFFECTIVENESS VS. EFFICIENCY

As we've already mentioned before, there is no point being efficient if you're working on the wrong things. You must practice being effective instead—i.e., you must focus your time and effort on the tasks that actually move the needle. Today, let's see how you can do that.

DAY 4—BEING STRATEGIC DURING YOUR DAY

Be strategic about productivity—do less exceptionally well, instead of doing more in an average way.

— LAURIE BUCHANAN, LIFE COACH AND AUTHOR.

Now that you have a better idea of what you want to accomplish this year and in the next 90 days, you can optimize your working day.

As a general rule of thumb, the more effective you are today and the closer it moves you to where you want to be tomorrow, the more productive you'll become. Makes sense, right?

Today, let's see how you can be more strategic during your day. The key is to remind yourself continuously that you must do the right things instead of doing things right.

Doing the right things means working on the key tasks you know will help you reach your long-term goals. These tasks are often the most demanding. They may even be a little scary. They may require a load of mental energy or they may be unpleasant, but strategic productivity requires you to complete these tasks until or unless you can outsource them effectively.

In truth, we usually know what we need to do—but we often fail to do so. For example:

- The writer knows that they should be writing more instead of spending too many hours interacting with readers on social media.
- The salesman knows they should be prospecting clients instead of tweaking their PowerPoint presentations for the umpteenth time.
- The aspiring coach knows they should be coaching more people instead of reading yet another book on coaching (though it may be necessary to a certain extent).

The strategic producer does the right things while the average person seeks to do things right. Therefore, you need to think hard. Identify your key tasks and work on them.

I. A 7-Step Method to approach your tasks the correct way

Now, to approach any task effectively, I recommend you follow the 7-Step Method as outlined below.

Step 1. Prioritize your task

Before you even start doing anything, ask yourself the following questions:

- If I could complete only one thing today, which task would have the most impact?
- Is this task moving me closer to my main goal?
- Do I really need to do this right now, or can I do it later?

You want to train yourself to think in terms of priorities and keep an eye on the bigger picture. Losing perspective and forgetting your overall strategy is the fastest way to waste time on unimportant tasks.

Step 2. Assess the validity of your task

To ensure the task is something you actually need to undertake, ask yourself the following questions:

- Do I really need to do this task?
- Is right now the best time? What will happen if I delay it for a week? A month? Forever?
- Am I working on this task because I need to or because it makes me feel good? Am I working on this task as a way to avoid what I really should be doing?

There is nothing more unproductive than doing something you didn't need to do in the first place. Answering the above questions can help you to avoid making such a mistake.

Step 3. Clarify what needs to be done

Before starting on a task, be certain you know exactly what is required. To do so, ask yourself:

- What do I need to do here?
- What am I trying to accomplish?
- What does the finished product look like?

You need to be specific. By knowing exactly what the output needs to be, you'll be able to optimize your approach and tackle the task more effectively.

Step 4. Determine whether you should be the person doing it

You have strengths, but you also have weaknesses. Whenever possible, try to delegate any task someone else can do better, faster or more cheaply than you. To do so, ask yourself the following questions:

- Is this task worth my time?
- Can someone else do it better than me? If so, can I ask for help?
- What will happen if I simply remove or postpone this task?
- Do I enjoy working on this task? Does it motivate me?

Little by little, you need to develop the habit of outsourcing everything you're not good at and focusing only on the high-value tasks at which you excel. Your time is more valuable than money. So, learn to use money to save time.

Step 5. Find the most effective way to tackle a task

As Abraham Lincoln said, *"Give me six hours to chop a tree and I will spend the first four sharpening the ax."*

Just taking a few minutes to consider the best way to approach the task can save you so much time in the long run. Ask yourself the following questions:

- What tools can I use, people can I ask or method can I rely on to complete this task as efficiently and effectively as possible?
- What skills could I learn to help me complete this task faster in the future?

For instance, let's say you've been asked to create a presentation at work. Rather than creating it from scratch, why not reuse or modify materials from a previous presentation? Always aim to utilize existing templates, methods, or knowledge. Be smart. The last thing you want to do is reinvent the wheel, right?

To sum up, before tackling any task, take a few minutes to work out the best possible way to approach it. This habit alone will save you a great deal of time and effort down the road.

Step 6. Batch the task with other similar tasks

Some tasks can be combined with other tasks that require the same type of effort or preparation. For instance, many YouTubers block one full day a week or even an entire month to record videos, as opposed to creating one video every day. This reduces setup time and makes the process far more efficient. Ask yourself:

- Can I batch this task with other similar tasks to boost my productivity?

Step 7. Automate your task

Finally, you should look for ways to automate your task, especially if it's a repetitive one. Ask yourself:

- Can I create templates to reuse every time I work on this or similar tasks? (For instance, you could design templates for the specific emails, presentations, or documents you need to create repeatedly.)
- Can I create a checklist? (Checklists provide you with specific steps to follow, making it less likely you'll forget a step or become distracted.)

Practice this 7-Step Method on a regular basis until it becomes second nature and you'll be able to use your time much more strategically.

Action step:

- Print out the 7-Step Method included in your action guide.
- Go through each step with at least one task today.
- Practice the 7-Step Method with more tasks until you've internalized it.

2. CEO/COO/Employee Framework

Another tool to help you be more strategic during the day is what I call the "CEO/COO/Employee Framework." This framework entails giving yourself different roles during the day to increase your strategic thinking and boost your productivity.

To explain it in simple terms, the CEO plans the day, the COO looks for ways to improve the system, and the Employee executes the tasks without overthinking them. The benefits of using this framework are as follows:

- **Removal of friction.** As you schedule specific tasks each day, you can move from one task to the next more easily, while reducing the risk of becoming distracted.
- **Decreased self-doubt.** This builds on the previous point. Since you've already decided what you'll focus on during the day, you'll be less likely to question your approach, work on unrelated tasks or become distracted. In other words, you'll give less room for your mind to come up with excuses.
- **Enhanced strategic thinking.** By taking time each morning to plan your day, you'll become better at thinking strategically. As a result, each action you take will be more effective.
- **Increased self-reflection.** As you dedicate a few minutes to reflect on your day, you'll develop more self-awareness.

By learning more about yourself and the way you work, you'll be able to optimize your work and boost your productivity.

Now, let's see briefly how you can start using the CEO/COO/Employee Framework today. To utilize this framework, you must plan your day each morning (CEO) while getting the buy-in of the Employee. That is, you (as the employee) should know:

* The specific tasks you'll work on,
* Why you must work on them (i.e., how does it fit your overall strategy), and
* How you will approach them for maximum effectiveness (refer to the 7-Step Method described earlier).

Having the buy-in of the Employee will make it easier for you to accomplish your tasks. If you doubt your ability or motivation to complete a certain task, take note of it and make adjustments by changing its scope, giving yourself more time, or eliminating it when relevant.

Finally, at the end of the day, assess how your day went (COO). Determine what went well and what could be improved. Perhaps you miscalculated the time needed to complete a task, or perhaps you approached a task in a suboptimal way. Or perhaps you procrastinated.

To conclude, planning your day will boost your productivity by ensuring you stay focused on your priorities. The more you follow the 7-Step Method and practice the CEO/COO/Employee Framework, the more strategic you will become, and the better the results you'll obtain.

To learn more about this framework, you can refer to my book, *Master Your Time*.

Action step

Using your action guide, practice asking yourself the following questions at the start of each day:

CEO:

- Exactly what tasks do I need to complete today?

Employee:

- Do I know how to complete the tasks?
- Do I have the skills or tools to complete them?
- Do I know *why* I need to do these tasks?
- Am I on board? Am I committed to doing them?
- If I feel inner resistance, what can I do to overcome it?

COO:

- What did I do well today?
- What could I have done better?
- What could be improved and exactly how?

Then, take a pen and a sheet of paper and write down the three main tasks you'd like to complete today and start work.

PART III

THINKING SMART

Part III. Thinking Smart

To make strategic productivity part of your life, you must practice thinking well. In this part, we'll see how you can achieve this.

People who ask themselves the right questions, build a more effective model of reality and achieve better results. This works as follows:

Smart questions —> effective thinking —> intelligent actions —> tangible results.

DAY 5—ASKING YOURSELF SMART QUESTIONS

Successful people ask better questions, and as a result, they get better answers.

— TONY ROBBINS, LIFE COACH AND MOTIVATIONAL
SPEAKER.

Today, we'll see how you can ask yourself smarter questions and why it matters. Whether you're aware of it or not, you ask yourself questions every day. These questions may be empowering or disempowering. Unfortunately, our self-talk tends to be fairly negative and the questions we ask ourselves often work against us.

Below are some examples of questions you may be asking yourself:

- Why do bad things always happen to me?
- Why am I so stupid?
- Why didn't I speak up during the meeting?

Obviously, these kinds of negative questions are unlikely to produce any insightful answers. Instead, you need to practice asking yourself empowering questions. Some of the best questions to ask yourself start with:

- How,
- What if, and
- Who.

Let's review some examples.

"How" questions

Rather than asking why something is happening to you, wouldn't it be more effective to ask yourself what you can do about it?

"How" questions help you become more result-oriented by focusing on ways to solve your problems rather than dwelling on them or blaming other people or situations. Some examples are:

- How can I prevent that situation from happening in the future?
- How can I become better/smarter or improve my performance?
- How can I make myself speak up during meetings?

Such questions help you brainstorm new ideas and develop solutions. Some more examples are:

- How can I achieve that goal faster?
- How can I accomplish twice as much while cutting my workload by half?
- How can I double my sales within the next six months?

Note that the more specific your questions are, the more detailed solutions you'll be able to create. The broader your questions are, the more creative ideas you might produce. Therefore, make sure you alternate between these two types of questions to get the best of both worlds. For example:

- How can I reach my goal as quickly as possible? (broad question).
- How can I reach that goal within thirty days while spending only ten hours a week working on it? (specific question).

"What if" questions

Your imagination is one of your most powerful assets. "What if" questions enable you to tap into it. They allow you to broadcast your desires to the world and set specific intentions. Here are some examples:

- What if I could design my ideal life?
- What if I could land my dream job?
- What if I could overcome my biggest fears?

Again, by making your questions more specific, you'll make it easier to find practical solutions:

- What if I could design my ideal life within the next three years?
- What if I could land my dream job within the next six months?
- What if I could overcome my biggest fears easily within the next 90 days?

"Who" questions

"Who" questions enable you to tap into the collective intelligence around you. There are millions of people smarter than you and who know how to achieve your goals. Why not ask them for help? Questions to ask include:

- Who has the answers to the most important questions I'm asking myself?
- Who has already achieved the goals I'm striving toward?
- Who embodies the qualities I want to cultivate?
- Who do I want to surround myself with?
- Who do I want to spend less time with?

Remember, your ability to tap into the collective intelligence can allow you to achieve far more than you would by yourself. Nobody is ever self-made. We all rely on previous technologies and millions of other people's work to reach our goals. Develop the habit of asking for help and aim to surround yourself with empowering people whether in real life or through books, courses, videos, or seminars. When I strive to achieve something new, I always ask myself the following questions:

- Who can answer my questions?
- Who has already achieved that goal?
- Who can share the most effective resources and/or tools with me?

If you develop the habit of asking yourself these questions, you'll save yourself loads of time and effort, and will become much more productive.

* * *

Action step

Return to your yearly goal and ask yourself smart questions such as:

- How can I achieve that goal faster?
- What if I could achieve that goal faster and more easily than I had imagined?
- Who has already achieved that goal or who knows someone who did?

Then, whenever necessary, practice asking yourself smart questions to improve your thought process, give yourself permission to dream bigger and achieve better results.

Keep the big picture in mind

One of the main reasons people fail to reach their potential is that they lose sight of the bigger picture. Although they have a specific goal or vision, they become distracted, which slows down their progress.

As we'll see tomorrow, they become victims of *Shiny Object Syndrome*, jumping from one activity, project, or goal to the next.

Another common issue is that we seek to keep the perfect balance between each area of our lives (career, finance, health, personal growth, relationships, et cetera). The problem with this approach is that we don't have enough time or energy to focus on all areas of our lives simultaneously. This is why it's usually more effective to pick one area and put most of our time and effort into it for several months. Once we've made satisfying progress, we can move on to the next area.

Think of a time when you tried to make many changes in your life. Chances are that you failed. It might have worked for a few weeks, but as soon as something unexpected happened, you started slacking off and reverted to your previous routines. The same thing happens when you undertake too many changes in too many areas of your life. The initial excitement might be intense, but it generally doesn't last.

As a *strategic producer*, you must focus on the key area that will unlock everything else. Often, it is your health. When you're healthier, you feel better and have more energy to work toward your goals. You also have more emotional space to challenge yourself and move beyond your comfort zone.

But if you're already healthy, perhaps it's your finance. Or perhaps you hate your current job, and this negatively affects other areas of your life. If so, you might need to focus on that.

Note that focusing on one area doesn't mean neglecting all the others. It simply means spending a disproportionate amount of time and effort on it for the greater good in the longer term.

So, if you were to improve one area of your life, which one would have the biggest overall impact on your life? Is it your health? Your career? Your finances?

* * *

Action step=

Using your action guide, become a strategic producer by:

- Identifying the one area of focus that would have the biggest positive impact in your life,
- Writing down the one goal you could focus on in this area, making sure it is specific and measurable,
- Writing down a simple action plan to ensure you make progress toward this goal,
- Focusing on this area until you attain satisfying results (usually for several months or even a year or more), and
- Moving on to the next area.

PART IV

LEARNING EFFECTIVELY

DAY 6—APPLYING WHAT YOU LEARN WITH MAXIMUM EFFECTIVENESS

In the end we retain from our studies only that which we practically apply.

— JOHANN WOLFGANG VON GOETHE, POET AND
PLAYWRIGHT.

Strategic productivity isn't about absorbing more and more information, it's about putting what you learn into action. In this section, we're going to see how to avoid the most common learning traps.

1. Finding the right information and applying it the right way

I believe there are two things you must do to reach almost any goal you desire. They are:

1. Being able to find the right information, and
2. Being able to implement the information to achieve tangible results.

If you continuously look for more information without taking enough action, you'll end up feeling overwhelmed and unable to make progress toward your goals. On the other hand, if you take action that isn't based on the right information or a sound strategy, you'll end up hustling without having many results to show for yourself. This is why you must balance these two components well.

2. Five learning mistakes most people make

Many people don't know how to learn effectively, and in a continuously changing world, your ability to learn and adapt to new environments or situations is critical to your success. Let's review the five mistakes that people make when trying to learn a new skill or when trying to achieve a challenging goal. These are:

A. Overlearning,

B. Analysis paralysis,

C. Illusion of competence,

D. Shiny Object Syndrome, and

E. Poor planning skills.

A. Overlearning

Being able to gather just the right amount of information is a skill that everyone needs to learn. Knowing the type of information to search for and for how long will make it easier for you to act. It will enable you to move toward your goals with more ease and achieve them faster. On the other hand, gathering too much irrelevant information—or information that is too detailed for what you're trying to do—is ineffective and will often lead to analysis paralysis.

To avoid learning too much, the first thing to do is define the scope of your research. It all starts by gaining clarity regarding the skills you're trying to learn and the goals you're trying to reach. For instance, if you're a Ph.D. student working on your thesis, you'll have to do far more research than if you're an employee asked to write a brief report on a topic. This is why you must always keep in the back of your mind:

- What you're searching for,
- Where to find it, and
- What the end product must look like.

In the first example, the Ph.D. student will need to read numerous books and research papers while, in the second example, the employee might just need to review a few articles or reports.

This may sound obvious, but many people fail to define the scope of the information they need to gather. They may also fail to establish a clear strategy of how to find it. Conversely, they use "studying" as yet another way to procrastinate.

What about you? What type of information do you need to gather to achieve your current goals?

Action step

- Select a skill you want to develop or goal you want to achieve.
- Now, write down what type of information you must look for and how you plan to do so for maximum effectiveness.

B. Analysis paralysis

Have you ever felt so overwhelmed with new information that you didn't know where to start?

This is perfectly understandable. We can only take in so much information at a time. When you try to bite off more information than you can chew, the result can be a sense of overwhelm often accompanied by a loss of confidence and motivation. Information overload leads to analysis paralysis for the following reasons:

a. You encounter contradictory information,

b. You start grasping the complexity of the topics, and

c. You lose sight of the big picture.

Now, none of the above points is a bad thing per se. In fact, in certain cases, it's necessary (if you're writing a thesis for instance). But if you're not careful, they can become huge hurdles, preventing you from learning effectively. Let's explain each of them briefly.

a. You encounter contradictory information

Finding the right information can be far more complicated than it first seems. If you don't believe me, think of all the conspiracy theories out there and how deep they often go. Sure, some of them may be (partially) true, but they cannot be all true at the same time. Or consider all the different weight loss diets available (Paleo, Keto, Atkins, Mediterranean, Vegan, and so on).

As you look for more data, you'll encounter pieces of information that directly contradict each other. The more you come across such information, the harder it will become to make a decision—and the less likely you are to take action (analysis paralysis).

For instance, imagine you're a sports coach, and you are trying to sell your first online training course. Looking for ways to sell lots of different courses, you listen to several marketing gurus. Great news! They all seem to have the magic pill you need. The problem is the pill is different each time. Examples of marketing tools include:

- Creating a Facebook group (marketer #1).
- Creating a YouTube channel (marketer #2).
- Doing podcast interviews (marketer #3).
- Getting a testimonial from an influencer in your field (marketer #4).
- Promoting your training course on social media (Instagram, Facebook, Twitter, or LinkedIn) (marketer #5).
- Creating more courses (marketer #6).
- Running Facebook ads (marketer #7).

This is a hypothetical example, but it goes to show you how easily you can become overwhelmed with advice.

We'll see later on how to deal with this issue effectively.

b. You start grasping the complexity of the topics

You can always go deeper with your learning. Many researchers spend decades on highly specific topics and still feel they've barely scratched the surface. For instance, some entomologists spend decades studying ants. Others dedicate their lives to the study of primitive cultures. To give you a more concrete example, I have a friend who has spent years studying hidden Christians in Japanese villages during the Edo period (1603-1868).

Now, in most cases, you don't actually need to know that much on any topic. When you first conduct research into a topic, your goal is to gain a decent understanding of it fairly quickly. But as you dig deeper, you'll perceive more nuances and grasp the complexity of the topic. The big picture will give room for tinier and tinier pictures. Soon, you'll find yourself unable to assemble all the pieces of the puzzle (i.e., the nuanced information you've gathered) to complete the puzzle (i.e., the big picture). In other words, you'll miss the forest for the trees.

As a result, you'll feel overwhelmed. The key is to identify whenever this happens. It's not that hard to spot. Simply observe yourself and see when things start to become confusing. Look for signs of frustration, loss of confidence, or lack of motivation. This often means that you're biting off more than you can chew. When this happens, take a step back, zoom out and refocus on the bigger picture.

For instance, imagine you're carrying out research for an article you'd like to post on your blog. You read through a couple of books you just bought. As you keep reading, you delve deeper into the topic. You understand more and more nuances and come across dozens of studies, countless stats, and various anecdotes. Inevitably, you begin to feel overwhelmed. Instead of gaining understanding about the topic, you become increasingly confused, unable to put the pieces of the puzzle together.

Now, a better way is to consume only relevant information, starting with simple articles or brief videos introducing the topic. Then, you can dive deeper if needed, but do it later.

The bottom line is, you must take in less information and take more action.

c. You lose sight of the big picture

When you try to absorb too much information, you risk losing sight of the overall picture. As you begin to see more detail, you'll find it harder to eliminate unnecessary information and retain only what you need. It all becomes blurry in your mind and you end up confused.

C. Illusion of competence

Another issue many people face when studying is what is referred to as "the illusion of competence". Put simply, this is the belief that you are learning—while in reality, you're not. Just because you spend hours doing something doesn't mean you're actually making progress. You can play tennis with your friends every

Sunday for years, but unless you actually set a clear intent to improve your game (e.g., by hiring a coach), you probably won't.

Whenever you learn something or work toward the accomplishment of a goal, be honest with yourself. Are you actually making progress? Are there ways you could make progress faster? As you do this, you'll realize that you tend to choose what's easy (and what makes you feel good), rather than what's effective (and difficult to do).

If you wish to learn faster than almost anybody else, you must do what's hard.

D. Shiny Object Syndrome

Do you keep jumping from one task to the next? Do you buy book after book or watch video after video without seeing any improvement? If so, you might be a victim of the *Shiny Object Syndrome.*

Developing *Shiny Object Syndrome* simply means you have difficulty sticking to something for long enough to achieve tangible results. Instead, you jump from one thing to the next like a kid who received (too many) new toys on Christmas day.

Shiny Object Syndrome is one of the main reasons people fall short of their objectives and fail to achieve any of their major life goals. Learn to overcome it and your productivity will skyrocket.

E. Poor planning skills

Another issue you might face is that you have failed to establish a specific learning schedule and strategy. As a result, you're disorganized, which makes your learning ineffective. For instance, you may be learning more than you need to or learning in a suboptimal way.

To avoid this mistake, you must ensure that you've identified exactly what you're trying to learn as well as the best way to go about it. This is what it means to be a strategic producer.

We'll discuss how to do this in the next section.

3. How to learn effectively

Now that we've covered the main learning traps, let's see what you can do to learn effectively.

To optimize your learning, you must reduce your input and increase your output. You need to absorb less information while taking more action on what you're learning. If you can do this, your ability to learn will dramatically improve. To stop overlearning, take a step back and define precisely:

1. **What you're trying to learn**, which will help you identify the type of information you need to gather and how deep you need to delve.
2. **Why you need to learn it**, which will help to ensure what you're learning is in line with your overall strategy.
3. **What the final result will look like.** Getting a clear picture of the final output will help you refine your approach. You'll be able to ask the right people, read the right books, and study more intelligently.
4. **The best way to learn it.** Once you've identified the best approach, you'll be able to design an effective plan of action.

For instance, let's say you want to learn a foreign language.

First, you need to decide what exactly you're trying to learn. Do you want to be able to have a conversation in that language? Do you want to read classics in that language? Or do you want to use it for business? Your learning approach will change depending on your goal.

For example, if you want to read books in a foreign language, you might spend more time studying grammar and reading as opposed to speaking. However, if you simply want to hold conversations in your chosen language, you'll need to concentrate on speaking rather than reading.

Second, you must also know your reason for learning it. How does it help you accomplish your goals? How does it align with your vision? When most of what you learn is a stepping stone toward the achievement of a bigger vision or dream, your motivation will be higher, and you'll be much more likely to persevere until you succeed in reaching your goals.

You'll be more motivated to learn a language if it's part of a bigger goal. For example:

- If you're eager to read the work of Solzhenitsyn or Dostoevsky in Russian, you might feel inspired to study Russian,
- If you're passionate about Japanese culture, you might feel the desire to learn Japanese, or
- You might be excited to improve your English if you love American movies.

Third, you must have a clear idea of what the final output will look like. In short, you must answer the question:

"Why am I learning this?"

In the case of foreign languages, you might ask:

"What will I use them for? Is it to read books? Make presentations at work? Watch movies in their original versions?"

If you need to carry out some research, what exactly are you doing this research for? What actual output is expected of you? Is it a five-page report? A fifty-page report? A PowerPoint presentation? What should it include? Exactly what are you doing it for?

When you're unsure, check with your supervisor or another relevant person. If you're the initiator, ask yourself what the final product should look like. Knowing this will help you identify the best resources (i.e., books you should buy, websites you need to visit, or people you could ask for help).

Fourth, once you know what you're trying to learn, why you must learn it and what the final output should look like, you can establish a detailed plan of action. You can determine the best way to learn that skill and the exact method you can use to achieve your learning goals.

To do so, sit down and take a moment to craft an effective learning strategy. Whether you need to find the answer to a simple question or carry out extensive research on a complex topic, it's always a good idea to take time to think instead of diving in headfirst. This simple practice will make you a much better thinker and help you become a great strategic producer over time.

4. Further specify your learning goals

Having a clear goal and a specific timeframe will motivate you to keep learning. For instance, when I was studying Japanese at University, I registered for the Japanese Language Proficiency Test. This test is held only once a year in Paris. It gave me a clear deadline and helped me define the scope of my learning.

Of course, you don't need to have an official deadline. You can set one yourself. For example, let's say you're learning Spanish. You could decide that you'll have a conversation with a Spanish friend on October 31st this year. To make it more effective, you can specify the scope of the conversation (i.e., self-introduction, travel experiences, and future goals).

The point is you must set crystal-clear goals to:

- Help you define the scope of your learning,
- Make your goal tangible,
- Inspire action,
- Create a sense of urgency using deadlines, and
- Enable you to design a well-defined action plan.

5. Identify the best learning strategy possible

Now that you've determined your goals, it's time to create the best strategy possible. As you do so, keep bearing in mind the overall scope of your goals. How much do you really need to learn? Do you need to read dozens of books or just a series of articles? Do you need to watch several videos or would it be enough to take one specific course?

To identify the best strategy, I encourage you to go through the following steps:

A. Find a friend or acquaintance who has already learned what you're trying to learn or who's already achieved the goal you're striving toward.

B. Ask yourself to identify the most effective way to reach your learning goal.

C. Create an action plan that maximizes your chances of hitting your target.

Let's discuss each point in more depth.

A. Identify a friend or acquaintance who has already achieved a similar goal.

The likelihood is, whatever you're trying to learn or achieve, someone else has probably already learned or achieved it before. Therefore, your first goal is to find that person and ask them for their "secret sauce". Of course, it doesn't mean you need to do the same thing or even that their method will work for you, but it's a good place to start. I encourage you to ask the following questions:

- What was your learning strategy?
- What was the single most effective activity for you?
- What did you struggle with the most and how did you overcome it?
- If you needed to learn that skill all over again, what would you do differently?
- If you were in my shoes, how would you go about learning it?
- Is there anything else I should know?

Once you have "interviewed" your friend or acquaintance, you should have a better idea of the best way to approach your learning goal.

B. Ask yourself to identify the most effective way to reach your learning goal.

Now that you've started to craft your learning strategy, let's go one step further. To do so, spend ten to fifteen minutes brainstorming ideas for strategies you could use to attain your goal. Below are some questions to ask yourself:

- How can I learn as quickly and effectively as possible?
- What should I avoid doing? (A good strategy requires you to reject most of the things you could be doing and focus on a very few high-impact tasks instead.)
- What does "overlearning" look like and how can I avoid it? What learning traps do I tend to fall into?

Make sure you come up with as many answers as possible.

C. Create an action plan that maximizes your chances of hitting your target.

Now that you have all the information you need to build a sound strategy, let's create a concrete plan. To define your action plan, ask yourself the following questions:

- What key daily activities are most likely to guarantee that I'll reach my goal?
- How much time do I need to invest to help me reach that goal?
- What are the main milestones along the way?

Action step

- Change your ratio of learning vs. doing by striving to do more and learn less.
- Select one learning goal and create a simple action plan. To do so, make sure you:
- Define exactly what you're trying to learn and its scope,
- Identify the best way to learn by conducting research and asking friends, and
- Create a simple schedule to make consistent progress.

6. Learning the right skills

What skills do you need to learn to reach your long-term goals? Leadership skills? Writing skills? Public speaking skills? Excel spreadsheet skills? And how should you prioritize studying them?

To be truly productive, you must learn the right skills. In this section, we'll discuss what I mean by the right skills and how to identify what these are for you.

Identify key skills you must learn

There is an almost infinite number of skills you could be learning, but your time is limited so you must choose well.

Now, learning skills is important, because the acquisition of new skills enables you to increase your productivity. As you practice a specific skill over and over, you end up doing a better job than the untrained person. In fact, this is what the "division of labor" studied by economists is all about. You can choose to do everything yourself—hunting, making clothes, building your house, et cetera—or you can focus on one or a few things you're good at while letting others provide you with everything else you need.

But what key skills should you learn and why? The answer depends upon what you're trying to accomplish. But that doesn't help, does it? So, let's review a few things before you start learning any skills. Below are the key components to take into account.

A. How does this skill help me reach my long-term goals?

To be truly strategic with your time and energy, you must use them to build the necessary skills to hit your goals.

For instance, if you want to be a writer but don't spend any time writing, you'll never reach your goal. Similarly, if you want to become a teacher but have poor communication skills, you'll struggle to teach no matter how knowledgeable you may be.

Now, think of a major goal you want to achieve. Then, ask yourself, "What specific skills do I need to develop to maximize my chances of achieving this goal?" Do you need to improve your sales skills? Writing skills? Leadership skills? Organizational skills?

To sum up, when it comes to strategic productivity, you must ensure that you identify the core skills you need to develop to reach your goals. Then, you must implement consistent habits and practical training systems to enable you to acquire these skills.

B. What skills will have the biggest leverage?

Not every skill carries the same weight. Some skills are more important than others. The most valuable ones are what I would call "meta-skills". Meta-skills can spread across several areas of your life and/or make the acquisition of other skills easier.

For instance, your ability to learn quickly and effectively is a meta-skill. Once you know how to acquire new skills or knowledge, it will have a positive impact on everything you learn, moving forward.

Meta-skills are really powerful.

I'd like you to think of meta-skills you could develop. Some examples are:

- **Learning how to study effectively.** Acquiring knowledge faster than anybody else gives you an enormous competitive edge in every single area of your life.
- **Communicating clearly.** Being able to share your thoughts and ideas clearly will enhance your influence, be it at work or in your personal life.
- **Listening attentively.** Being fully present and listening carefully to people will enable you to improve the quality of both your personal *and* your professional relationships.

What about you? If you were to acquire or further develop new skills, which ones would have the biggest impact on your long-term productivity?

Remember, developing just a couple of skills can dramatically improve your productivity—and your life.

C. What skills act as bottlenecks? What skills leverage your strengths?

Whenever you seek to acquire a new skill, you make trade-offs. In other words, when you choose to learn a skill, you also choose (indirectly) not to learn other skills during that same time.

This is why you must be strategic. Should you improve on what you do poorly? Or should you put all your effort into improving what you're already good at? The answer will vary, depending upon your goals. In general, I believe it's more effective to focus on your strengths. However, in some situations, you might be better off working on your weaknesses. Here is how to think about it:

When to focus on your strengths

Keep focusing on your strengths whenever you're already seeing positive results. If you're unsure what your strengths are, look at areas in which you're getting positive results or feedback.

For instance, when I released my first book on Amazon, I received a lot of positive feedback. As a result, I decided to dedicate a large chunk of my time to writing more books. However, if the feedback had been overwhelmingly negative, I would probably have given up and focused on something I was better at.

On the other hand, I'm not great on camera. Other people would obtain far better results with far less effort. As a result, I chose not to spend too much time on improving my speaking skills (for now).

When to focus on your weaknesses

Focus on your weaknesses when they become obstacles standing between you and success. For instance, if I decide today that I want to appear on dozens of podcasts to increase my visibility and sell more books (which, I believe, is a pretty decent strategy), I will spend more time improving my communication skills.

Or imagine someone whose brother died from a drug overdose and who made it their mission to help kids stay away from drugs. If they chose to deliver their message to schools across the country, it would make sense for them to overcome their shyness and/or poor communication skills.

What about you? Are there any bottlenecks that stand between you and success? If so, do you need to address them?

You might also want to focus on your weaknesses when they negatively impact your self-esteem. For instance:

- If you need to do presentations at work and feel terrible every time you stand in front of an audience, working on your presentation skills might be a good idea.
- If you feel ashamed of yourself because you can't use Excel properly, improving your spreadsheet skills might be a smart move.

The bottom line is this. Work on your weaknesses when they're clearly an obstacle or when they affect your sense of self-worth. Otherwise, consider ignoring them or have someone help you out by delegating or outsourcing these tasks whenever possible.

D. How many skills should you focus on?

Your time is limited and so is the number of skills you can learn. I wouldn't recommend you focus on learning more than two to three new skills at the same time. Some examples of valuable skills are:

- Coaching,
- Decision-making,
- Leadership,
- Logical thinking,
- Marketing,

- Persuasion,
- Public speaking,
- Sales,
- Writing, and so on.

Again, whatever skills you choose to cultivate, make sure they are aligned with your goals. By combining two or three skills and achieving a high level of proficiency in each, you can gain a competitive edge over most people and carve out your own path.

For instance, there are many great independent writers and there are many great marketers, but very few writers are also good marketers. These are usually the ones who end up being the most successful (i.e., selling the most books).

Become excellent at the two or three most important skills needed to reach your goals, and you will be well on your way to attaining them.

* * *

Action step

- List all the skills you need to learn to reach one of your biggest long-term goals.
- Select the two or three skills that will have the biggest positive impact and will maximize your chances of reaching that goal.
- Then, rank them in order of importance.

Additional tip:

When looking for skills to focus on, make sure they inspire you. Unless you're motivated, it's unlikely you'll reach an expert level in any skill.

7. Further considerations when learning a new skill

Whenever you choose to develop a new skill, consider the level of expertise you need to acquire. Your time and energy are limited. Therefore, there is no point in becoming overly good at a skill that is only partially useful or one that isn't needed at all.

This is important because the gap between being good and being an expert is enormous. While you may reach eighty to ninety percent proficiency at a skill relatively quickly, acquiring the last ten percent might take you years. There is a difference between:

- Being able to have conversations in five languages and being an interpreter for the United Nations,
- Being really good at soccer, basketball, and baseball and being an NBA player, and
- Being able to play a few songs with the piano, the guitar, or the bass and being a violinist in the Vienna Philharmonic.

In short, you can learn multiple skills at the same time it will take you to reach the expert status at one thing.

Therefore, be highly selective with the few skills you want to master and avoid spending more time than needed on things that will only bring marginal results (unless you love doing it, perhaps).

PART V

MANAGING YOUR ENERGY

DAY 7—MANAGING YOUR ENERGY WELL

Life begets life. Energy creates energy. It is by spending oneself that one becomes rich.

— SARAH BERNHARDT, ACTRESS.

Today, we're going to see why learning to manage your energy well is critical. We'll also discover how to do so. The more energy you have, the more productive you will become.

1. Using peak time effectively

We all have periods during the day in which we have far more energy than we do at other times. During these times. we think more clearly, are more inspired, and do better work as a result. Unfortunately, many people fail to maximize this window of opportunity. Instead of working on key tasks, they waste time chatting on social media, checking emails, or completing minor tasks. If they repeat this behavior day after day, they will destroy their focus and kill their productivity.

Don't be like them. Instead, use your peak times to focus on your major tasks. Remember, productivity isn't about time—it's about focus, clarity, and energy levels. One hour of focused work during your peak time can be worth many hours of work at other times. As you keep tackling key tasks when you have the most energy available, your productivity will increase dramatically.

While we're all different, for many of us, our peak hours occur during the morning. If you're unsure when you have the most energy during the day, run the following simple experiment:

Select a challenging task that requires a lot of energy. Then, work on it in the morning one day, in the afternoon the next day, and the evening the day after that. See when you have the most energy and mental clarity and note when you produce the best output.

The bottom line is this. If you can identify your peak hours and make sure you work on key tasks during these hours, your productivity will skyrocket.

2. Using diffused mode and focused mode effectively

You've got to hustle, grind and work your face off to achieve success and make Uncle Gary Vee proud of you, right? (Gary Vee/Vaynerchuck is a well-known entrepreneur who posts loads of motivational content online). Working hard is certainly necessary at times, but I believe it's far more important to work *intelligently*. This entails having a clear strategy and knowing what you're good at and what you should delegate.

In truth, you can only focus for a few hours each day. To be productive you must alternate between "push" and "pull" periods.

During push periods, you remain focused on your main work trying to get as much done as possible.

However, during "pull periods", you let go and relax. You stop trying so hard and let your subconscious do the work. You allow your mind to come up with creative solutions and innovative ideas. To relax you can:

- Ask a question of your subconscious and let go,
- Chat with a friend or colleague,
- Perform relaxation or stretching exercises,
- Go for a walk,
- Grab a coffee,
- Meditate,
- Practice breathing or mindfulness exercises, or
- Sit and do nothing.

The point is you must alternate between focused work periods and periods when you simply relax and do nothing. This gives your brain time to process information and consolidate your learning or provide you with valuable insights.

Also, note that the more creative work you do, the more important it becomes to alternate between diffused and focused mode.

3. Carving out time to think each week

I'm also a great believer in the importance of carving out time to think each week. This is because I'm convinced that "busyness" is usually the result of lazy thinking. It's the price we pay for refusing to take enough time to think and plan. Now, thinking doesn't mean:

- Dwelling on the past,
- Worrying about the future,
- Seeing yourself as a victim,
- Complaining,
- Trying to validate your current beliefs (political or religious beliefs),
- Making quick assumptions, or
- Repeating what you've heard from so-called experts.

Instead, it means (among other things):

- Confirming you're moving in the right direction,
- Reflecting on what you could have done better,
- Optimizing your processes to boost your productivity or enhance your well-being, or
- Brainstorming innovative ways to skyrocket your success in various areas of your life.

Spending an hour or two each week doing strategic thinking might be one of the best uses of your energy. For instance, it might help you find better solutions to your problems and save you tons of time. Sometimes, you're merely one simple idea away from changing your life or growing your business exponentially. Carving out thinking time during the week increases your odds of coming up with such a killer idea.

4. Segmenting your day

Busy people go from one task to the next all day long. They have no time to breathe and tend to be overstressed. Worse, they may even multitask, which many studies have shown to be ineffective.

On the other hand, productive people are much more *intentional* with their day. Rather than hustling and bustling, they strive to complete key tasks. They focus on doing the right things, not doing things right.

Remember, the energy you have each day is limited. While skipping breaks may sound like a good idea, it usually isn't. To become a strategic producer, you must take rest breaks between focused work sessions. You must be deliberate, knowing at all times why you're doing what you're doing.

Let me give you one example.

Person A works all day long barely taking any breaks.

Person B determines exactly what they will focus on and works with intense focus for forty-five minutes before taking a fifteen-minute break. Then, they repeat the process.

Now, who do you think will be the most productive? Person A or Person B?

You might think Person A will be the most productive. However, in the real world, Person B will be more deliberate and focused and, as a result, more effective. Taking frequent breaks will allow Person B to recharge their battery and to get ready for the next work session.

On the other hand, Person A will tend to waste time on minor tasks or become distracted. Not taking breaks, they will feel more tired, which often leads to poor decision-making (i.e., working on ineffective tasks, making more mistakes, et cetera). Person A will also experience more stress and will likely end up feeling overwhelmed.

This is why I encourage you to segment your day. To do so:

- Decide what to work on. Set specific goals for the day and for each work session.
- Take regular and ample rest breaks between each work session.
- Stay focused on your main work. Whenever you notice yourself being distracted, make a conscious effort to refocus on your task.

Segmenting your day will help you use your energy much more effectively and will reduce the risk you'll feel stressed or overwhelmed. Try it out for yourself! You'll be stunned by how effective it is.

* * *

Action step

Using your action guide, rate yourself on a scale from 1 to 10 (1 being false and 10 being true) for the following:

- I make the most of my peak time every day.
- I use "diffused mode" and "focused mode" effectively.
- I carve out time to think each week.
- I'm intentional in the way I run my day, and I segment it effectively.

CONCLUSION

You can be busy, or you can be productive. The choice is yours.

In a world where we have access to more information than we can possibly absorb, our ability to craft a crystal-clear strategy, find the right information, and take effective action until we reach our goals, is our superpower.

In the past seven days, you've made significant progress toward becoming a strategic producer. Now, it's very likely you'll become distracted sooner or later. You might chase the next shiny object, or you might get lost in meaningless tasks that don't move you any closer to your goals.

But this is okay.

It's part of the process.

When this happens, take a step back and look at the forest—not the trees. Refine your overall strategy, refocus and take consistent daily action to move you toward the vision you want to create. Remember, people who have a clear vision and specific plan of action will almost always achieve more than people who don't.

How could it be otherwise?

Therefore, create a solid plan, find the best strategy and identify the most impactful actions you could take to reach your goals.

Then, using the content from this book, develop the mindset of the strategic producer. Whenever you face a new task, ask yourself whether it's really the best use of your time. If you do this consistently, over time, you'll become one of the best strategists you know. More importantly, you'll reach most of your goals, even the ones that seem difficult or perhaps impossible right now.

It's now up to you to perform the work and achieve the results you aspire to. I can't do the work for you, but I can wish you all the best in your future endeavors.

Thibaut Meurisse.

PREVIEW - DOPAMINE DETOX (BOOK 1)
A SHORT GUIDE TO ELIMINATE DISTRACTIONS AND TRAIN YOUR BRAIN TO DO HARD THINGS

Tell me if this is you:

You know that if you could tackle just one specific task, it would have a massive impact on your overall levels of productivity. Perhaps it would improve your chances of earning a promotion. Or perhaps it would enhance your mental or physical well-being.

But you never seem to start.

Instead of working on your goal first thing in the morning, you end up checking your emails, looking at your stock portfolio, or scrolling your Facebook newsfeed instead.

Soon enough, that important task will appear less and less appealing. You tell yourself you'll just have one more coffee. Or you'll click on just one more YouTube video. But the more you delay your task, the harder it becomes to get started. It's as though an invisible mental barrier had appeared between you and your task, and this barrier seems impossible to overcome.

Have you ever felt this way?

If so, you'll greatly benefit from this book. In it, we'll introduce a simple method you can use to avoid overstimulation and make it easier to tackle your key tasks.

So, are you up for the challenge?

In **Part I. Dopamine and the Role it Plays**, we'll explain what dopamine actually is and how it works. After reading this section, you'll understand why you can't stop checking your phone, struggle to stay away from social media, or binge-watch videos.

In **Part II. The Problem**, we'll see why dopamine can be an issue these days. In this part, you'll discover how your dopamine transmitters have been hijacked and why this can be a major challenge.

In **Part III. The Benefits of a Detox**, we'll review all the reasons a dopamine detox can be useful. We'll introduce a number of different types of dopamine detoxes and we will discuss several misconceptions regarding dopamine.

In **Part IV. A Three-Step Method for a Successful Detox**, we'll explain in detail how you can implement an effective dopamine detox in three simple steps.

In **Part V. Doing the Work (and Overcoming Procrastination)**, we'll focus on getting you back to work. In this segment, you'll learn how to plan your day effectively and remove distractions to help you remain focused.

Finally, in **Part VI. Avoiding "Dopamine Relapse"**, we'll work through some simple tools and techniques to help you avoid overstimulation and stay focused on your key tasks over the long term.

Let's get started, shall we?

DOPAMINE AND THE ROLE IT PLAYS

You've probably heard about dopamine before and have at least a vague idea of what it is. In this section, we'll briefly define dopamine and describe the role it plays.

Dopamine is a neurotransmitter which makes us anticipate rewards such as having sexual relationships or eating nourishing food. Dopamine gives us the desire to take action to earn the exciting reward that's waiting for us. It is the force that makes us act. As such, it is a very useful neurotransmitter that has helped us survive and reproduce—and probably one of the main reasons you and I exist today.

Contrary to what many people believe, dopamine is *not* a pleasure chemical. Simply because an event triggers the release of dopamine doesn't mean it is something we like or get pleasure from. In fact, when you pay close attention, you'll notice that as soon as you obtain the expected reward, you'll often feel empty and unfulfilled.

The truth is that no amount of stimulation will ever bring you the sense of fulfillment you're seeking. Yet, many of us are constantly overstimulated, looking for the next source that could trigger a release of dopamine. It seems as though we always want more and are never satisfied. And the more we seek stimulation, the worse it becomes.

Now, look at your own life. What are you addicted to? What do you crave? What are your main sources of stimulation? Do these things really make you happy?

As you consider these questions, you'll probably notice that you're addicted to highly stimulating activities (such as watching video games, immersing yourself in social media or reading emails). When you undertake these activities, you start losing self-control —you want more and more stimulation. And even though they may not give you any real pleasure or lasting fulfillment, you keep doing them. After all, you need the next hit of dopamine, don't you?

Under such a state of stimulation, any task that requires concentration becomes much harder to perform. As a result, you will procrastinate. You delay writing that book you've always planned. You put off starting that new venture, or you'll postpone that key project you're in charge of.

To sum up, from an evolutionary perspective, dopamine's role is to encourage you to act to earn the anticipated reward needed for your survival or reproduction. This is dopamine's primary role. Unfortunately, in today's world, the process has been hijacked, which leads to many unintended consequences, as we'll discuss in the next section.

To read more visit the URL below:

mybook.to/dopamine

ACTION GUIDE

I. Planning Effectively

Day 1 - Planning your year

First thing you need to consider: what would make the next twelve months truly valuable?

Now, visualize yourself in exactly twelve months from today. Then, write down what you would have accomplished by filling in the prompt below:

The last twelve months were truly amazing because:

_____

Now, that you've written down some of the things you'd like to achieve, select just one of them. To help you identify the one thing you'd like to focus on, answer the questions below:

What is one thing that if I achieve this year would make me proud of myself?

_____

_____

What is the one thing that if I achieve this year would make the biggest positive difference in my life?

_____

_____

What's one thing I've always wanted to do (but haven't)?

_____

_____

What do I really really want?

_____

_____

_____

_____

_____

What's the one thing that scares me the most? (What scares you is often what you need to do the most?

_____

_____

Finally, use the space below to plan the next twelve months

Day 2 — Making the dominos fall

Time to identify the right domino(s) you need to collapse in order to maximize the odds you reach your goal. To help you with that, consider the following:

1. What one thing would enable you to build the most momentum?

_____

2. What new paradigm(s) could you adopt?

3. What one thing or specific strategy would have the biggest possible impact and allow you to make the most amount of progress?

4. What one thing would reduce your field of options and make almost everything else easier or unnecessary?

Day 3 — Planning your ninety days

Set your ninety goals.

Look at your yearly goal and identify the milestone(s) you must hit to reach it. Reverse-engineer the process. To do so, ask yourself the following question, "what would I need to have completed by Q3 to ensure I'll hit my target? What about Q2? Q1?

Write down the key milestone(s) for each quarter with as much details as you can. Don't try to create a perfect plan. Just do your best. You can also refine the process later on if necessary.

II. Planning Effectively

Day 4 — Being strategic during your day

Step 1. Prioritizing your task. Ask yourself the following questions:

- If I could do only one thing today, which task would have the most impact?
- Is this task moving me closer to my main goal?
- Do I really need to do this right now, or should I do it later?

Step 2. Assessing the validity of your task. Ensure the task is something you actually need to undertake. There is nothing more unproductive than doing something you didn't need to do in the first place.

- Do I really need to do this task?
- Is right now the best time? What would happen if I delay it for a week? A month? Forever?
- Am I working on it because I need to or because it makes me feel good? In short, am I working on this task as a way to escape from what I really should be doing?

Step 3. Clarifying what needs to be done. Be certain you know exactly what is required. By knowing exactly what the output needs to be, you'll be able to optimize your approach and tackle the task more effectively.

- What exactly do I need to do here?
- What am I trying to accomplish?
- What does the finished product look like?

Step 4. Determining whether you should be the person doing it. Whenever possible, try to delegate any task someone else can do better, faster, or more cheaply than you.

- Is this task worth my time?
- Can someone else do it better than me? If so, can I ask for help?
- What would happen if I simply remove/postpone this task?
- Do I enjoy working on this task? Does it motivate me?

Step 5. Finding out the most effective way to tackle a task. Consider the best way to approach the task can save you so much time in the long run. Ask yourself the following questions:

- What tool(s) can I use, people can I ask, or method can I rely on to complete that task as efficiently and effectively as possible?
- What skill(s) could I learn to help me complete this task faster in the future?

Before tackling any task, take a few minutes to work out the best possible way to approach it. This habit alone will save you a great deal of time and effort down the road.

Step 6. Batching the task with other similar tasks. Some tasks can be combined with other tasks that require the same type of effort or preparation. This reduces setup time and makes the process more efficient.

- Ask yourself: Can I batch this task with other similar tasks to boost my productivity?

Step 7. Automating/systemizing your task. Finally, you should look for ways to automate or systemize your task, especially if it's a repetitive one. Ask yourself:

- Can I create templates to reuse every time I work on this task or similar ones? (For instance, you could design templates for the specific emails, presentations, or documents you need to create over and over.)
- Can I create a checklist? (Checklists provide you with specific steps to follow, making it less likely you will become distracted.)

The CEO/COO/ Employee Framework

Try giving yourself different roles during the day to increase your strategic thinking and boost your productivity. Practice asking yourself the following questions at the start of your day:

CEO:

- Exactly what tasks do I need to complete today?

COO:

- What did I do well today?
- What could I have done better?
- What could be improved and exactly how?

Employee:

- Do I know how to do the tasks?
- Do I have the skills/tools to complete them?
- Do I know why I need to do these tasks?
- Am I on board? Am I committed to doing them?
- If I feel inner resistance, what can I do to overcome it?

Then, take a pen and piece of paper and write down the three main tasks you'd like to complete today and begin to work.

III. Thinking smart

Day 5 — Asking yourself smart questions

A. Go back to your yearly goal and ask yourself smart questions such as:

1. How can I achieve that goal faster?

2. What if I could achieve faster and with more ease than I had imagined?

3. Who has already achieved that goal or knows someone who did?

Then, whenever necessary, practice asking yourself smart questions to improve your thought process, allow yourself to dream bigger and achieve better results.

Keeping the big picture in mind

One of the main reasons people fail to achieve as much as they could is because they keep losing sight of the bigger picture. While they have a specific goal or vision they'd like to move toward, they get distracted along the way, which significantly slows down their progress.

B. Identify the one area that if you were to focus on, would have the biggest positive impact in your life.

1. Write down what one goal you could focus on in this area. Make sure it is specific and measurable.

2. Write down a simple action plan to ensure you make progress toward this goal.

3. Keep focusing on this area until you get satisfying results (usually for several months or even a year or more).

4. Then, move on to the next area.

IV. Learning effectively

Day 6 — Being strategic during your day

Overlearning

Select a skill you want to develop or goal you want to achieve. Now, write down what type of information you must look for and how you plan on doing so for maximum effectiveness.

Create an action plan that maximizes the odds you hit your target.

1. Change your ratio learning vs. doing by striving to do more and learn less.

2. Select one learning goal and create a simple action plan. To do so, make sure you:

a. Define exactly what you're trying to learn and its scope

b. Identify the best way to learn it by doing research and asking friends

c. Create a simple schedule to make consistent progress.

Identify key skills you must learn

1. Write all the skills you need to learn to reach one of your biggest long-term goals

2. Select the two to three skills that will have the biggest positive impact and will maximize the odds you reach that goal

3. Put them in order of importance

Additional tip: when looking for skills to focus on, make sure they inspire you. Unless you're motivated, it's likely you'll reach the expert level in any skill.

V. Managing your energy

Day 7 — Managing your energy well

Rate yourself on scale from 1 to 10 (1 being false and 10 being true) for the following:

1. I make the most of my peak time every day

0 _____ 10

2. I use diffused mode and focus mode effectively

0 _____ 10

3. I carve out time to think each week

0 _____ 10

4. I'm intentional in the way I run my day and segment it effectively

0 _____ 10

Notes:

Notes:

Printed in Great Britain
by Amazon

81095324R00068